Body as Tool

By

Tracy Lybbert

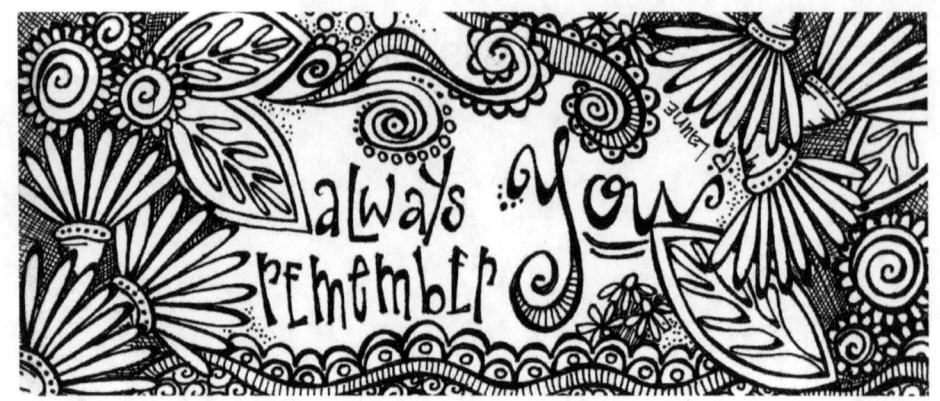

Theatre Anywhere

Empowering your student while learning at home

Theatre and You!

Theatre is a place that looks and feels different from other courses and classrooms and a place to take a deep breath, laugh, live, and enjoy the performance arts. Theatre is a place where we observe life, relationships, and events and gives us an opportunity to see things from different perspectives, cultures, and time periods. Drama is the foundation of all schooling and prepares participants with the communication and team building skills necessary for life.

Theatre is Activating

Theatre engages the whole brain in play making it an important self regulatory and brain stimulating class for all students.

There are five primary functions of the brain[1]:

- Strategic planning
- Memory and recall
- Analytical thinking
- Creativity and imagination
- Kinesthetic learning.

---

[1] Based on Tedxtryon by Denis Medued "Changing your brain can be as simple as child's play"

Theatre Stimulates All 5 Brain Functions

- Planning an improvisation is a form of strategic planning. Performers use their mind, body, voice to move on stage, and create scenarios.

- Memory and recall. Performers build on skills, use the imagination, sense recall and character building techniques in game and performance opportunities.

- Analytical thinking. Students reflect on the parts of an activity by discussing what they liked, what was confusing, summarizing the game, and giving a one word description of the game. Students learn how to critique live and filmed performances.

- Creativity and imagination. Students actively participate in games, variations of the games, scripted performances and improvisation material which stimulate the imagination and creative play.

- Kinesthetic learning. Many games will emphasize different senses and movements supporting participants in feeling embodied and engaging others in meaningful play..

Theatre is a fun class that also prepares you for life! It is a place to learn about different people and places, a time to be with friends. We learn how to listen and respond, how to manipulate space and use body language appropriately. We learn about our actions and consequences and vicariously about those in plays. As science explores creativity, we are learning the importance of being together in co-regulatory play and the beneficial nature of relationship in a creative space - drama!

This self study guide should support you in starting a theatre curriculum in a virtual or home school experience and give you a chance to play and laugh, and be connected to your friends, your space, and your body. Find appropriate ways to connect online in a space with friends and family to play the games in this guide.

Navigating through this guide should be easy. Each lesson starts with an introduction to the skill, then a game is played to reinforce the concept and get some experience incorporating the daily focus into an activity followed by simple reflection. You may choose one activity for a day, or all the activities for a day. Do what you need to do in a way that makes sense to YOU! Enjoy!

The Body as Tool
Theatre Anywhere

Your student guide to mastering Theatre while learning at home

This unit will give you a break from a virtual classroom and get you moving and actively using all of you to feel embodied, awake, and ready to learn while teaching you how to use your body effectively on the stage. How? The body is the performer's tool and the fundamental aspects of using our body effectively on stage is to understand what messages are being sent to us, what messages we create in our body, how we convey those messages to an audience, and then incorporating the acting space to relay that message to the audience.

You will engage all of your senses and practice ...
Listening and receiving information,
Listening to your body messages,
Moving your body through space in new and different ways,
Understand body language, and
Use space effectively as a performer.

By the end of this unit, you should be aware of your physical body and the variety of ways you can move while responding to other people, locations, and stimuli which establishes the basic skills of a performer to use their body as a tool on stage.

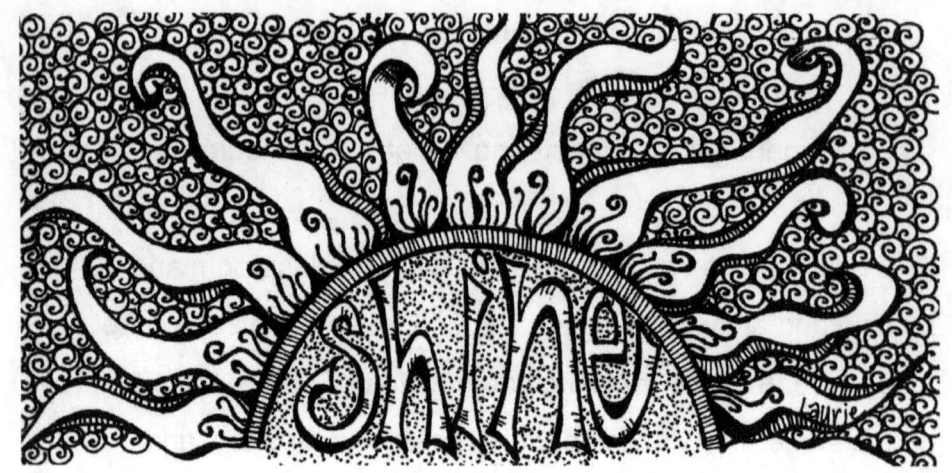

The body as tool

Lesson Plans

Lesson 1
Responding to External Sounds

Lets begin

What are the sounds you have heard today? When you think about receiving this sound, what does it feel like coming into the ear, how do you receive it in your mind? How does it travel through your body? Does this sound affect your environment?

Let's stand up and think of one word that stops us from really listening, maybe its distractions, overwhelm, boring, confusing…. Say this word out loud. Take your right hand and just pat your left shoulder and place your left hand on your right shoulder and just pat both shoulders.

What would be one word that supports us in really listening? Maybe its interest, focus, concentrating, fun, me .. what one word comes to mind? Say this word out loud and as you are patting your shoulders just pat down both your arms until your hands are clapping and then place both hands on your feet and pat up both your legs till your hands are clapping again. Very good!

Gather a friend or family member to play a game

Narration One person says a story to another person. When they are done, the second person says, What I hear you say is … (*give a simple summary of their story*) ... Did I understand this right?" Give the first person time to say yes or no and what was missed. Then the second person tells a simple story to the first person who then gives a summary and asks if they heard it right.

Red Light Green Light One person stands on one side of the room and the rest of the class stands on the other side of the room. When the person turns their back to the group they say "Green Light" and the other performers start walking toward this person. When the leader turns around they say "red light" and the group must stop walking. If the leader sees movement, the name of the moving student is called and they go back to the beginning to attempt walking undetected toward the leader again. The game ends when a person from the group reaches the game leader, touches their shoulder. Then they get "to be it" and lead the movement listening game.

Horse Shoe Everyone sits or stands in the shape of a U. The two people at the tips of the U are the leaders. The person on the left starts a rhythm and then the person directly behind them begins creating that movement and sound as well, then the person behind them begins and so on until the entire U is making the sound. When the first person on the far right is the last person adding to the rhythm, they change it creating a new beat for everyone to follow. This person makes a sound, then one by one, each person behind them begins making the sound. Then when the person at the front of the line on the left side receives the sound and begins to create it, they, then change the beat and create a new sound wave one by one, and so on.....

Pause and reflect

Take a moment to stand up and stretch up tall, and shake one leg then shake the other leg. Hop back and forth shaking your arms, shake your head and your hips and your whole body. Listen to the sounds around you. Take a moment to thank the friends in your group for playing the games and give one complement!

Lesson 2
Remembering body movements

Lets begin

How is your day going? What movements have you done? (For instance: wake up, eat, get to school/work.)

Have some regular day activities on 3X5 cards such as making a sandwich, getting dressed, packing a school bag. Have participants choose one of the cards and **Play Charades**. One person will act out the activity and others will guess what it is.

Often we do the exact same movements every day, and with theatre, we want to do games and activities that get our body moving and listening in different ways so that we can use all of ourselves as "the performers tool".

Gather a friend or family member to play a game

First lets play a game that incorporates listening and how that sound is received and decoded through our body mind system.

Listen to understand. Someone says a statement. The next person says as you say …. I wonder about ….. Then the first person says "hearing you wonder about … makes me wonder about ….." What is the internal movement in your mind as you hear people talk.

In the next game, let's be silent and concentrate on the movement of the body in a game.

Mirror Game Two performers stand face to face about an arms length apart. Then they bring their palms up about shoulder height with palms facing each other but not touching about 3 inches apart. One person begins movements, and the other person is the mirror following the movements. After a couple minutes, change and have the other person lead.

Balloons. Blow up balloons and have everyone move around the room. They have to keep the balloons in the air without using their hands. No one can touch each other or use their hands. Imagine there is no gravity and you are floating through space keeping up the balloons, how does that change your body movements?

Pause and reflect

Everyone lay down and close your eyes, gaze down, or find an object and soften your focus. How still can you lay and allow all thought, sound, and movement, to drip into the ground and just feel the gravity holding you firmly to the earth. When you are ready, wiggle your fingers and toes, blink and look around the room and move back into your regular school day.

Lesson 3
Responding to internal stimuli

Lets begin

Sometimes we aren't really curious and aware and listening, and oftentimes our bodies go through the same motions every day in basic routines. There are usually tasks or jobs that must be done and we learn to focus and perform them. In theatre, we want to reharmonize the body to be able to listen, move, and understand the messages we are receiving from our body and really be alive in the moment and able to adjust our activities as needed!

Gather a friend or family member to play a game

Find a Truth. Everyone sits in a circle. The first person says, "What is true for me right now is …" *(they give a simple action)* such as "I want to stretch" or "I want to yawn" or "I want to pat myself on the shoulder." If this is true for anyone else in the circle, then they follow along with this action as well. To review, the first person says a truth, then the group may all join in doing the simple action.

Then the next person says "what is true for me right now is …(*simple action*) and others can follow along if they would like.

This game is an important part of my virtual classroom and supporting my children at home, because, when we are doing school work, if I see or sense they are getting frustrated, I say, "What is true for you right now?" Because of the game, they can tap in pretty quickly to what they are feeling and needing.

Breathe. Breathe in 8 seconds, hold. Breathe out 8 seconds, hold. Right index finger blocks right nostril breath in 8 seconds, hold. Breathe out 8 seconds, hold. Relax the right hand. Left index finger block left nostril, breath in 8 seconds hold. Breath out 8 seconds hold. Relax both hands and simply take a breath. Breath in 8 seconds, hold. Breathe out 8 seconds, hold.

Play "twister" or try **Person to Person** Write different body part labels on 3X5 cards such as "foot" "elbow" "wrist" "shoulder" "back". Two players will be on the stage or in the playing space. One person will draw two cards and then say them such as "foot" to "elbow" the two people on stage then have to connect. For instance, if foot and elbow were called, One person puts their foot to the other person's elbow. This is a quick moving game and a fun one to get performers to think and listen with their body and mind.

Pause and reflect

Take a moment to discuss the way your body is feeling and what is the truth for you after participating in the theatre lesson. Listen to each other and give each person a compliment.

Do a full body shake out by shaking your head and your shoulders, then your torso and arms, shake your hips and legs all the way down to your toes!

What is true for you right now? What do you need to do before you go to the next class, or move into the next part of your day?

Circle Art

Draw pictures and write words that reflect your learning in this theatre uni on using your body as the actor's tool.

Lesson 4
Understanding the messages we send

Lets begin

In virtual meetings, our facial expressions and body language seems minimalized. The physical cues we send out, are not noticed or not seen. I can then find myself not fully present if I am answering the door or talking to a family member. It is like my body goes into a freeze mode and sometimes feels weird coming out of it and actually talking to a person.

So let's stand up and just stretch up to the sky on the inbreath and let your arms come out and around down to your side on the outbreath. Then breath in and squeeze your thigh muscles and breath out pushing your heels into the ground. Now place your hand on your heart and breath in and breathe out.

Everything we do sends messages to others. We may be in a virtual meeting, reading a book, walking down a path, or talking with someone. Every situation sends messages by things such as our clothes, postures, and facial expressions.

Gather a friend of family member to play a game

Walk stop justify The performers move around the room in different ways *(such as moving in jello, no gravity, popping corn).* The performers want to move their body as unusually as possible to explore different ways the body can move. After a few movements of movement exploration, one person will say "freeze." Performers need to stop and freeze like a statue in a unique way. Everyone stops as they are and takes a turn telling an explanation or reason for why they are standing in the position they are.

I am a Tree This is a game where one performer stands on the stage and makes a body position and gives a statement to justify it. They may stand on the stage straight with arms extended upward and say, "I am a tree." A second performer comes up onto the stage and has to add to the stage picture by creating a physical posture, and a statement to add to the narrative or story. Perhaps the second person comes on the playing space and makes himself into a ball and says "I am a rock." Then a third person comes onto stage and creates a position and statement such as I am the man standing between a rock and tree.

Then the first player chooses one of the other players to exit with them. The person left on the stage restates what they are; perhaps it was player 2 who stayed who will say "I am a rock" and then two new people will come onto stage creating a new story line. This game moves fast and is one of my children's favorites. It is a low effort game but increases their energy and they laugh.

Pause and Reflect

The way we walk, stand, look, and express ourselves with our hands and facial expressions tell a story. As we learn who we are and how our body responds, we then learn who others are and how their responses send messages deeper than words.

Say one thing that you appreciate about yourself and find someone today that you can compliment. Watch their body language when they receive a good statement!

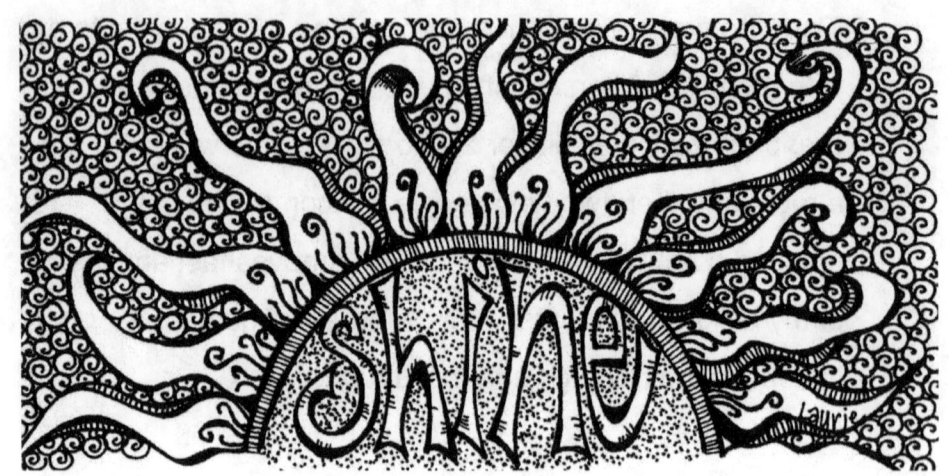

Place a picture of you performing here

Lesson 5
Using Space

Lets begin

How do you use your space in a virtual classroom? What if you lean into the camera or move away from it? What are interesting ways to enter or exit the screen? From above or below? From side to side? What are the perspectives of people who view you on the screen?

Now think about you in a room with people. How close do you sit? How fast do you walk? How are items in the room arranged? How do you move around the furniture?

Have you ever designed or decorated a room or a set for a play? Can you recall different places you have been and how you might recreate them on stage? Everyone can close their eyes, look down to their knees, or just find an object in the room and soften their gaze. Invite yourself to be curious about what you can recall about the space around you right now. Open your eyes and see how close you were to remembering the details in the room.

Gather af friend or family member to play a game

Step 1: Have everyone walk around the room and spread out as much as possible. Then, make a boundary so the space is smaller and everyone has to move round a small boundaried area without touching each other. Move the playing space back to normal size and have everyone continue walking around.

Step 2: As everyone is slowly walking around, have participants look and be aware of each other. Ask everyone to be curious and to make eye contact with each person they move past if this is appropriate for them. Next, ask each participant to greet each other as they are moving and walking around this space. How do you say hello to people you pass by?

Step 3: Now ask participants to imagine a grid. Each student walks on a grid so all movements are straight lines with 90 degree angle turns. Turn as often as possible, and then delay the natural response to change directions for as long as possible. Try walking as slow as possible, and as fast as possible and then back to regular speed.

Step 4: Allow the group to relax their movements and walk around the classroom and just explore space. Then call out "Freeze" When the participants hear this, they stop moving. Then the person calls out a number such as 3. The participants then get into groups of three. The person calling out can use any number for any size group.

Play defender Have the students walk around the room and privately, without telling anyone, choose someone to "defend them" and one person "to avoid". Participants do not tell anyone who they have chosen as avoider and defender. Each participant must move carefully and do their best to keep moving around the space, keeping the defender between them and the person they are trying to avoid.

Reflection

Close your eyes or soften your gaze, try to imagine the space you are in and what you can recall? Open your eyes and see how accurate your memory was!
Movement supports our ability to observe and remember during our school day!

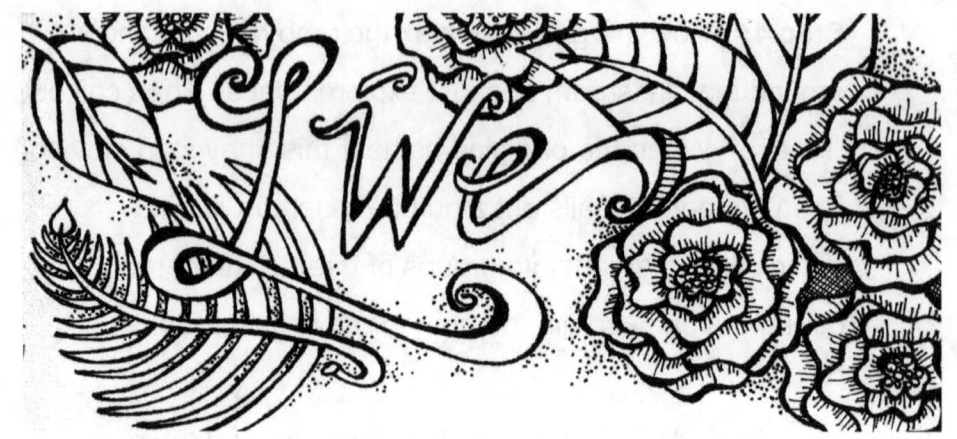

Theatre Anywhere by Tracy

While learning at home, or in a virtual classroom, incorporating theatre into your day will bring joy, self regulation, and embodiment for improved learning experiences.

The Body as Tool

The body is the performer's tool and the fundamental aspects of using our body effectively on stage is to understand what messages are being sent to us, what messages we create in our body, how we convey those messages to an audience, and then incorporating the acting space to relay that message to the audience.

You will engage all of your senses and practice …

Listening and receiving information,

Listening to your body messages,

Moving your body through space in new and different ways,

Understand how our body movement and internal messages communicates, and

Use space effectively as a performer.

By the end of this unit, you should be aware of your physical body and the variety of ways you can move while responding to other people, locations, and stimuli which establishes the basic skills of a performer to use their body as a tool on stage.

Staging Secrets

Staging Secrets includes The Power of Movement and gives you a variety of games and teaching ideas to support students in moving intuitively and effectively on stage supporting the confidence of students in owning the stage floor. How do you cover technical details of movement and still keep performers honest and authentic on the stage? Using game play and simple framing devices for learning creates the learning modules you need for student success.

Students will …..

Respond to sounds, music, images, and the written word, incorporating movement,

Identify theatrical vocabulary, including basic anatomy of theatre spaces,

Demonstrate safe use of the voice and body, and

Identify and apply audience etiquette at all performances.

By the end of the unit students will be able to …

Respond to images words sounds with movement,

Identify theatre vocab, and

Demonstrates use of voice and body.

Power Up Your Performance!

Say Yes! To the moment. Say Yes! To winning. Say Yes! To bringing all of your unique vast life experiences and personality into every engaging theatrical experience. Power up your performance looks at the basic building blocks of creativity including observation, concentration, listening, character building techniques and more. Enjoy exploring acting skills through game place and scene performances.

In this unit students will …
Develop characterization based on sensory and emotional recall,
Dramatize literary selections and imitate life experiences, and
Develop simple observations about theatrical performances.

By the end of the unit students will be able to …
Develop characterization,
Dramatize selections, and
Develop oral and written observations.

Character Magic!

From Written Word to Great Performances.

This guide reveals the craft of bringing characters to life on stage, from super-secret script analysis to jaw-dropping, opening-night performance. Uncovering facts from the script, imagining the greatest wants and desires for the character and bringing it all together in a magnificent performance is made easy in this unit. Script analysis becomes an effortless and easy process of discoveries within these lessons laced with game play and peer support.

This guide will lead you on a journey to learn ...

- How to make an authentic character
- Responding to the environment making things real
- Revealing action strengthening character
- Knowing your character wants and getting them
- Finding the whys for character actions
- Making all of this come together to make your character shine

By the end of this unit, you will be able to describe your character, the relationships, and their environment.

Keys to Characterization

Unlocking the power of you to shine bright on stage

Unlocking the power of you to access all of yourself and create unique characters with simple character building steps.

Keys to Characterization will give students an overview of script analysis and acting techniques to get on stage and shine bright. Teachers have a clear set of instructions that create engaging and flexible lessons that make sense to administrators, teachers, parents, and most importantly to the students who are practicing skills toward great performances.

Students will power up their performance as they study .....
Internal and external conditions of the character,
Gestures, mannerisms and stretching a character,
Goals, obstacles, and motivations of a character, and
Observation, focus, listening, and energizing a scene.

By the end of this unit, you will be able to effectively portray a character during performances.

Improvisation Magic!

We are born with this desire to learn, and to struggle, and feel joy in the learning process. When we do improvisation we tap into this innate joy for life and the process of growth!

Improv uses all our theatre muscles to get us to think quick, build scenes and plays, work with our team members, and laugh at our mistakes. Theatre, especially improvisation, teaches us to learn from our choices, and always say yes moving toward growth and joy!

In this unit students will….

Express emotions and ideas using movements and dialogue, and Identify and apply audience etiquette at all performances.

By learning about …

Characterization,
Ensemble Work,
Physicalization,
Pantomime,
Props,
Entrances and Exits, and
Gibberish.

Structure for Strength

This guide gives you a foundation for creating improvisation and identifying play structure. The lessons in this guided journey supports you in learning different ways you can perform and how to create meaningful coherent work.

In this unit you will experience...
How to build an improvisation,
Identify the structure in scenes and plays,
Understand different types and styles of dramatizations, and
Identify and apply audience etiquette at all performances.

By the end of this unit, you will be able to…
Perform any scene directing the energy of the play in harmony with the playwright's intent, and
Be able to create your own scenes in a coherent way that an audience will understand and enjoy.

Tracy Bradley

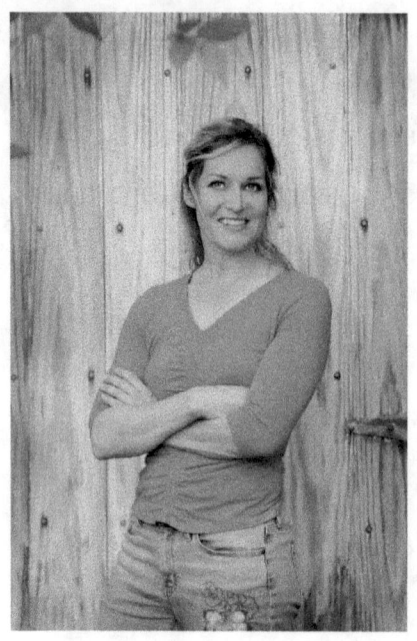

My first teaching assignment was Harker Heights High School in Central Texas. I wanted to develop a program in the way I wished I had been taught. I realized my high school experience was mostly creative and college was mostly intellectual resulting in a loss of enthusiasm. I desired to create a program that balanced left and right brain activities while creating a bridge between the two skill sets keeping students actively engaged in the theatre process.

My program balances games and scene work with cognitive skills reflecting through art and words. I developed habit and skill assessments and also encouraged a way of memorizing that created the integration necessary to keep students creatively courageous on stage.

Next I taught in a title one environment and developed the warm up technique which is a guided imagery with a golden light to support this fundamental need. I then experienced teaching in a very different school in the area expanding this warm up technique into side coaching and the performances were phenomenal -

There you have it.

Left and Right Brain integration for balanced learning
Memorization technique for full embodiment of character
Informal and formal assessments based on skills
Rehearsal and Performance assessments based on habits
Warm Up technique for accessing the power of YOU to shine in life and on stage. Enjoy!

www.ingramcontent.com/pod-product-compliance
Lightning Source LLC
Chambersburg PA
CBHW050324220526
45465CB00005B/2118